Sporty Lou
Soccer King

By Quentin Holmes

This is the tale of a mighty soccer king. Years before his real-life soccer fans will cheer and sing. Today is the day it will all begin. The dawn of a champion, a mighty legend.

Who is this future soccer king? The one who will hold this famous claim? A mighty kid will do it; Sporty Lou is his name.

Sporty Lou, 'The Legend.' Sporty Lou, 'The Proud.' Sporty Lou, the greatest sports star of them all! Outside in his backyard Sporty Lou is the boss... well, next to his mighty dad of course!

© 2017 Holmes, Investments and Holdings, LLC.
All Rights Reserved
No part of this publication may be reproduced, stored in a retrieval system, or transmitted, in any form or by any means, electronic, mechanical, photocopying, recording, or otherwise, without the written permission of the author.
This book is a work of fiction. Places, events, and situations in this book are purely fictional and any resemblance to actual persons, living or dead, is coincidental.
Printed in the United States of America

ISBN: 978-0-9992369-5-6

His dad says, "Son, I will teach you with pride a game I learned when I was your age."

Sporty Lou looks confused, arms stretched out by his sides. Why is his dad so serious? What does he have in mind?

Suddenly his dad's serious face bursts into an awesome grin. A ball appears from behind his back, all black and white from end to end. The ball has a shine that mirrors the sun. If this is going to be the game, Sporty Lou can tell that it will be fun.

"This was my very first ball. I used it as a boy. Now, I'm passing it on to you to enjoy!" Sporty Lou had seen this before; it was like the one on TV. Kicked all around, from town to town, by some of the world's greatest athletes!

Now at last it is Sporty Lou's time. He doesn't know the rules, but he is ready to try. He loves the smell of the grass, so strong and so sweet. The ground feels so bouncy beneath his two feet.

Suddenly, in his mind Sporty Lou's backyard disappears. In its place is a huge soccer stadium where fans yell and cheer.

Over the crowd Lou hears his dad give the call. "Alright son, get ready, here comes the ball!" He is so nervous, his little legs can hardly stand. But inside his imagination, Sporty Lou is the man!

Just as the ball approaches, he grabs it with both hands! The crowd yells as they rock back and forth in the stands. He raises his two hands, now waving to the crowd. They are cheering his name and the cheering grows loud.

His dad shakes his head. "No son, I'm sorry, but that's not how you compete. Rule #1 of soccer is to always use your feet! You cannot grab the ball unless you are the goal-keep. So line up again and let us repeat."

The crowd's loud cheers now turn into disappointed moans. His fortune and fame are now stuck on permanent pause. He begins thinking "this game might be kind of hard." The referee blows his whistle and holds up a warning yellow card

But he is determined; he'd never give up so quickly. Sporty Lou stomps his little feet, bites his lower lip, and prepares once again to give the ball a kick.

The ball comes towards him. It's moving very fast. He reaches out for a moment, but then remembers not to use his hands. Half of the crowd gasps as the other half sighs. In anxious anticipation, he closes his eyes.

He pictures the perfect kick that will send the ball flying high through the air, but when he opens his eyes he can't see it anywhere!

Dad shakes his head, "Rule #2 my son, the ball can be tricky. You've got to watch it at all times. It move very quickly!"

True to those words and just that fast, he turns around and sees the ball that rolled past.

Sporty Lou 'The Mighty' now begins to frown.
Sporty Lou 'The Legend', is now feeling let down.
The crowd is restless, they begin to moan and complain. The opposing team laughs at his shame.

Sporty Lou 'The Mighty' is almost ready to quit. It's over, it's hopeless; both he and this game are a terrible fit. How can a game this hard possibly be fun? If things don't change quickly, Sporty Lou 'The Legend' will surely be done.

But his dad simply smiles, like there's a special secret that only he knows. Perseverance is the food that makes greatness grow.

"You can do it Sporty Lou, don't give up. I believe in you!" If his dad says he can do it, then Lou believes he can too.

Sporty Lou lines back up, prepares to see this task through. His opponents line up too, the stadium full of fans chanting: "Lou! Lou! Lou!!!"

As the ball begins to roll, the rules appear in his mind. "No hands, only feet and watch the ball at all times."

Sporty Lou pushes his foot forward, using all of his might. Will he do it this time; can he finally get it right?

"Boom!" is the sound as he kicks the Ball! "Boom!" just like a rocket leaving the ground. Instantly he falls in love with the sound!

The crowd is going crazy; his dad jumps up and down! Sporty Lou leaps so high in the air, his feet are in the clouds!

This is so much fun; Sporty Lou doesn't want it to end. He loves the feeling of playing; he loves the feeling of the win.

And even as the sun sets down and the day's end is near, Sporty Lou is still shouting, "Come on dad, let's play it again and again and again!!!"

www.ingramcontent.com/pod-product-compliance
Lightning Source LLC
Chambersburg PA
CBHW042100290426
44113CD00003B/111